The Positivity Tribe

by Christopher J. Wirth & Chris Wilberding

The Positivity Tribe

Copyright © 2021
by Christopher J. Wirth / Chris Wilberding

Printed and Electronic Versions
ISBN: 978-1-7354093-2-0
(Christopher J. Wirth / Chris Wilberding /
Motivation Champs)

To order additional copies or bulk order contact the
publisher, Motivation Champs Publishing.
www.motivationchamps.com

Christopher J. Wirth

I dedicate this book to Zachary, Emily and Mason. I love you three very much. The Sky is the limit - Dream Big!

Chris Wilberding

I dedicate this book to Team Wilberding. Thanks for your support, encouragement, and love. Not just now, but always.

Love you!

Praise for The Positivity Tribe

"*The Positivity Tribe* is a must read for anyone looking to bring more positivity into their life. Staying positive isn't as easy as it sounds, this book makes it a lot easier. Together, we all can positively impact the lives of others, and this book shows you how."

Brian Cain
MPM, Mental Performance Coach

"*The Positivity Tribe* demonstrates that being positive is a choice you can make. Something as seemingly insignificant as an anonymous handwritten note can ignite positive change for those around you. Positivity is contagious... share this book with everyone you know! You will be glad you did."

David Cottrell
Author, Monday Morning Leadership

"A fantastic story about the power of positivity. '*The Positivity Tribe*' demonstrates the value of turning challenges into opportunities. This book will resonate with audiences of all ages. Grab yourself two copies - one for you and one to share."

Jon Gordon
Best-selling author of The Energy Bus and The Power of Positive Leadership

"*The Positivity Tribe* is a reminder that the most effective ideas and stories do not need to be complex. This fable will encourage you and reaffirm that the best way to combat overwhelm and despair is to be kind to others, one person at a time and one day at a time."

Matthew Del Negro
Actor, Podcaster (10,000 Nos)

"I love the simplicity of the what *The Positivity Tribe* represents. The power of positivity is real, and it is possible - one person at a time. Well worth the read, and I encourage everyone to continue to spread positivity."

Damon West
Author of The Change Agent, Bestselling co-author of The Coffee Bean

---

"*The Positivity Tribe* hits on a very important topic, the power of positivity. A wonderful story that needs to be shared with the masses. Grab yourself a copy!"

Pat Williams
Basketball Hall-of-Famer, Author of Leadership Forged in Crisis

FOREWORD

I am truly honored and privileged to write the foreword to a book that represents the power of positivity and the impact that it has when it's payed forward. Christopher Wirth and I met at the University of North Carolina back in 2000. He was an AAU basketball coach for the Connecticut Flame and I was an assistant basketball coach for the Tar Heels. Being a New Yorker, I immediately gravitated to his grassroots basketball team. Christopher and I continued our friendship throughout my college coaching career. Our conversations about basketball would eventually turn into discussions on leadership, teamwork, and accountability. He was always curious to hear how our coaching staff implemented these concepts into our programs.

Christopher was also an avid reader and loved to hear about the last book you had read. If he thought a note, phone call, or a book would be of some value, he would never hesitate to share. In 2004, I received my first Coach John Wooden book on leadership and a note from Christopher that read "Spread Positive Energy." I've spent the past two decades watching Christopher evolve and grow into one of the most dynamic coaches on positivity and leadership. Christopher's commitment to spreading the power of positivity is phenomenal! His daily motivational messages through social media platforms, podcasts, positivity notes, and "We Rise By Lifting Others UP" forums are amazing. Through his guidance, we started a weekly call of thought leaders that connect and collaborate on how we can intentionally impact and make a positive difference in all areas of our lives. I know first-hand that Christopher understands the power of positivity and gratitude, especially during times of struggle, challenging, and adversity.

I was fortunate to have the privilege of meeting Chris Wilberding through Christopher, and we immediately connected. At first the connection I had with Chris was based upon his positive mindset and how he approaches each day. Over the next few weeks we continued our conversations and a sincere friendship was formed. We later found out that we both knew many of the same people from Chris' basketball coaching days. I am honored to call Chris a friend. It is very obvious to me why Christopher and Chris immediately connected and decided to collaborate on this fantastic book.

The Positivity Tribe is an inspirational tale about three high-school students dealing with negative experiences. Everyone has faced obstacles throughout their lives. This book gives you the blueprint on how to turn a negative mindset into a positive mentality. You will discover the impact of positivity and how it not only affects you but the power it has over others.

The Positivity Tribe reminds us that constantly complaining and griping fuels unhappiness and negativity, but repeated acts of kindness and gratitude attracts people and things for you to be thankful for.

I use *The Positivity Tribe* as a resource on the importance of focusing more on serving others. It has helped me to be more intentional with my daily actions empowering as many people as I can, one person at a time. It's a reminder that when you treat people well, they in turn treat you better!

The Positivity Tribe gave me a game plan on how to extend myself outside of my household. The Community Service Wednesday is something that really hit me.

Thanks to this book, my local telephone pole has turned into the community "Positivity Pole" filled with notes of love and gratitude.

I challenge each reader to pay it forward with positivity in their own way.

Fred Quartlebaum
Director of Basketball Operations
University of Kansas, Men's Basketball

Introduction

In August of 2019, while searching for MORE positive content to continue his personal development, Chris Wilberding had the good fortune of discovering the No Quit Living podcast and immediately became hooked on every episode. Not only did Chris find outstanding content and great guests, but he also had an immediate connection with the No Quit Living mission and more importantly it's founder Christopher J. Wirth.

Their connection was solidified when they realized that there was only one degree of separation between them and their professional experiences. They had much in common from being former college basketball coaches to having young kids and ultimately the desire to make a positive change in the world - one person at a time.

Since initially connecting, they have partnered to spread positivity via multiple social media outlets, began coordinating and hosting a positivity-focused weekly mastermind with another friend all while continuing the spreading of positivity. This has resulted in sharing positivity to 10s of thousands of people throughout the United States and around the world. Mainly focusing on students from elementary through high school and a rapidly growing list of colleges/universities.

As they release their first book together *The Positivity Tribe: Power of Positivity - One Person at a Time*, they believe that the themes of positivity, togetherness, and community will inspire people of all ages and the young at heart to develop a positive mindset and bring positive energy to others in every aspect of their lives.

We hope that you enjoy *The Positivity Tribe* and its story of how when people come together they can achieve great things.

Chris Wilberding

CHAPTER 1:
In the Hall

A typical start to a Monday at West Gordon High School. The junior class hallway was abuzz with students heading to and from their red lockers which lined both sides of the bright white hallway. Everyone was getting ready to begin another busy week of school.

Mike sauntered down the hall towards his locker with a disappointed look on his face. He opened his locker which happened to be next to the lockers of his two best friends—Jennifer and Pete. He mumbled something under his breath.

"What was that, Mike?" Jennifer asked.

"Nothing. I just wasted all that hard work over the summer and this fall. I'll be spending my junior basketball season, once again, on JV this year," Mike answered with a smirk.

"I'm sorry, Mike. If it makes you feel any better, I'll switch places with you but then you will have to deal with those four girls that are constantly calling me names and picking on me," Jennifer said.

Pete was listening to this brief exchange and decided to chip in. "At least the two of you get a break after school. That's usually right about the time I get brought into my parent's on going divorce," Pete said as he closed his locker.

The janitor, Mr. Williams, approached Jennifer, Mike, and Pete and made sure to make eye contact with them. With a warm and inviting smile he said, "Good morning Jennifer, Mike, and Pete. I hope the three of you have a great day."

A bit startled, Jennifer, Mike, and Pete all managed to politely smile and acknowledge Mr. Williams as they continued down the hall to class.

That afternoon, Jennifer, Mike, and Pete were all sitting across from each other on the bus.

"Everyone, take your seats so we can get out of here!" the bus driver said loudly over the buzz of multiple conversations taking place.

Jennifer, Mike and Pete sat in silence for a couple of minutes.

"I'm glad today is over," Mike said distinctly.

"Ya, me too," Jennifer repeated.

"Well, if either of you would like to trade places and go to my house to witness my parent's painful divorce firsthand, I would gladly trade places." Pete responded sarcastically.

"Deal! I'll go to your house, but then get to experience those four girls constantly bullying and teasing you on a daily basis," Jennifer frowned.

"One of you should take my basketball home with you, as clearly I won't be needing it anymore" Mike chimed in sarcastically.

Jack, who was seated in the next row turned around to face Jennifer, Mike and Pete. "Thank God the three of you are getting off at the next stop because you guys are killing me with your negativity." He shook his head as he turned back around.

Jennifer, Mike, and Pete sat in silence. A couple of minutes later the bus came to a halt. Jennifer, Mike and Pete all got off the bus and walked towards their houses without saying a word. As she approached her driveway Jennifer looked at Mike and Pete and very quietly said, "See you guys tomorrow."

"See ya," Pete responded.

"Have a good one," Mike followed.

Chapter 2:
The Morning Bus

The next morning Jennifer was already at the bus stop as Mike and Pete approached. When the bus parked the three made their way to the back. As they approached their usual seats, they heard Jack mumble, "Oh good, it's the negativity crew."

Jennifer, Mike, and Pete looked at each other and silently took their seats. They sat uncomfortably quiet for the rest of the bus ride.

Upon arriving at school, they each went their separate ways to begin the morning.

Chapter 3:
Character Challenges

As Jennifer approached her locker in the junior hallway, she, once again, saw the four girls in her class who had been bullying her pointing and laughing. This had been going on since last year, and Jennifer wasn't sure how much more she could take. She chose to ignore the girls.

Mike approached the entrance to his first-period class and saw three of his junior classmates that made the Varsity Basketball Team dribbling a ball and discussing last night's practice. Mike quickly walked into the classroom before he was spotted.

As Pete was heading into math class his phone vibrated. A text from his mom. It read "Your father rescheduled his dinner plans with you again. Please order yourself something for dinner. I should be home by 7:30." Pete shook his head and walked into the classroom.

Chapter 4:
The First Three Notes

Jennifer walked out of the girls' bathroom and headed towards her locker. As she opened her locker, she noticed a white note. It said: "Believe in YOU. YOU have GREATNESS in YOU." She immediately turned around to see if anyone was there. She was alone in the hall. Jennifer reread the note three more times before she put it in the front cover of her book and walked into history class, a huge smile on her face.

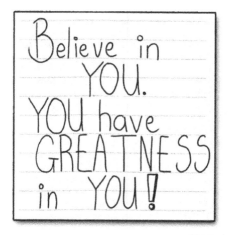

Pete and Mike were walking down the hall together to their lockers. Mike turned to Pete and said, "I'll see you on the bus later."

"You got it," Pete replied.

Pete needed to get his book for English class. He opened his locker and there was the same size note that Jennifer had in her locker with a message written in black sharpie. The note said "Everything is going to work out. Spread Love and Hope Today."

Pete thought Mike was messing with him. He turned toward Mike, but Mike's head was in his own locker as he was reading what looked like the same type of note himself. Mike's note read, "Never give up on your goals, YOU got this!"

Mike quickly turned around, Pete was faced the other way and holding what appeared to be his own note in his hand. Both Mike and Pete closed their lockers at almost the exact same time and headed in different directions to their classes. Mike turned to Pete and said, "See you later."

Chapter 5:

"The Positivity Tribe" & "Positivity Notes"

The afternoon bus pulls up to school and the students take their usual seats as multiple conversations ensue. Two stops later Jennifer, Mike and Pete all get off quietly and begin walking in the same direction to their houses.

Jennifer turned to Mike and Pete with her "Positivity Note" in her hand. "Ok, which one of you put this in my locker?" she asked.

Almost in unison Mike and Pete pull their own "Positivity Note" from their backpacks and held them up with smiles on their faces.

"Ha, I was sure both of you gave me my note." Mike said.

"Nope, I actually thought the two of you were the ones that put my note on top of my English book." Pete replied.

"Hey guys, I have to help my mom with some stuff, but can the two of you come over to my house after dinner?"

Jennifer asked.

"That works," Mike said.

"Bet, we'll see you there," Pete said.

A few hours later, Jennifer, Mike and Pete were sitting at the kitchen table in Jennifer's house talking and eating ice cream. Jennifer turned her chair to face Mike and Pete. "Do you guys remember when Jack called us the 'the negativity crew' a couple of days ago on the bus?"

"Ya, I didn't like it" Pete responded.

"Me neither" Jennifer said. "I know the three of us have been dealing with some stuff this year but being labeled the 'negativity crew' didn't sit well with me."

"Not at all," Mike followed.

"What if we decided to really make a positive difference?" Jennifer suggested.

"What do you have in mind?" Pete asked through a mouthful of ice-cream.

Holding her "Positivity Note" Jennifer said, "I am not one hundred percent sure, but when I opened up my locker and found this note, it genuinely changed my mood. Right before lunch, I got bullied again, and I was in a dark place."

Shaking his head Mike says, "Honestly, my note put me in a much better frame of mind for the rest of the day."

"Me too. I received a sarcastic text from my mom criticizing my father once again, and I was having a bad day." Pete said.

"What if the three of us did something together?" Jennifer asked.

"I'm all ears." Pete shot back.

"Think about the positive impact the notes we received had on us individually. Prior to that the three of us were having a rough day," Jennifer said.

"That's true." Mike said.

"What if we made some sort of pact together? To hold each other more accountable to be more positive not only towards each other but to others as well?" Pete followed.

"I like that," Jennifer said with a smile.

"The Positivity Tribe! That's what we'll call ourselves!" Mike blurted out.

"THE POSITIVITY TRIBE"

"The Positivity Tribe... I like the sound of that. And why don't we pass out our own 'Positivity Notes' all over school?" Pete said.

"That is awesome, maybe we could even spread some notes in town and throughout the community," Mike added.

"Our motto will be – We Rise By Lifting Others Up!" Jennifer said.

"WE RISE BY LIFTING OTHERS UP"

"Yes, and our goal will be to positively impact one person, one note at a time," Mike said with a huge smile on his face.

"The three of us doing this together is going to be fun," Jennifer remarked.

"Ya, it will, and together we are going to be able to have a huge impact on so many people," Pete said.

"Ok, everyone put your hands in, together on three. One, Two, Three," Mike said and the three of them shouted, "TOGETHER!"

Jennifer pulled out a large thick pack of computer paper, grabbed some scissors, and sharpies. Mike grabbed his phone and turned on some music. For the first time in what seemed like a while, the three of them were just having fun. They weren't thinking about getting bullied, not making the team or their parents' divorce. They spent the next two hours laughing, having fun and smiling as they looked up positive and inspirational quotes and messages for their "Positivity Notes."

Chapter 6:
The Bus Stop the Next Morning

Jennifer approached the bus stop the next morning. She was early and the only other person already waiting for the bus was Jack. With her "Positivity Note" in hand, Jennifer asked, "Were you the one that left this in my locker?"

With his eyebrows scrunched and a look of surprise, Jack responded, "Nope, that wasn't me."

"Well regardless, I wanted to thank you for letting the three of us know that our negative attitudes were becoming a bit too much."

Mike and Pete approached the bus stop from down the block.

Jack continued, "I was honestly only trying to help."

"I appreciate your honesty." Jennifer admitted.

"I am sure we have all heard our parents say it a thousand times, but honestly really is the best policy," Jack replied.

The bus squeaked down the street and came to a stop.

Jennifer nodded, "That is true, honesty is very important."

Jennifer, Mike, Pete, and Jack all got on the bus.

"HONESTY IS THE BEST POLICY"

Chapter 7:

Jennifer Reaches Out

Jennifer was walking down the hall to her history class when out of the corner of her eye she saw the same four girls that had been bullying her picking on another girl in the junior class. The four girls were laughing, and one of them pushed the girl softly on her left shoulder and scoffed "loser" as they walked away. Jennifer knew how the girl must be feeling and she felt the need to do something. As she approached the girl, Jennifer could tell that she had been crying. Jennifer quietly asked, "Are you ok?"

Without lifting her head up or making any eye contact, the girl very quietly whispered, "Yes."

Jennifer knew that the girl wasn't ok. Jennifer delicately put her hand on the girl's shoulder and said, "I know you probably want to fight back, but revenge is never worth it."

Lifting her head to make direct eye contact with Jennifer, the girl said, "I didn't do anything to them."

"I know, and neither did I. I want to share something with you that I think might help. People who are hurting, hurt people. I know it might not make you feel better, but those girls are hurting themselves. Unfortunately, they are taking their pain out by bullying the two of us. It isn't right and it doesn't seem fair, but the reality is that deep down inside those girls are probably in a lot of pain."

"HURTING PEOPLE HURT PEOPLE"

"I honestly never thought about it that way before," the girl said. "I know you also didn't have to stop and check on me. That was really cool."

"I've been in your shoes before, and at times I felt alone. I'm just glad I was able to help."

"Thank you," the girl said with a genuine look of appreciation on her face.

Jennifer smiled and handed the girl a "Positivity Note" as she gave her a hug. The girl looked down at her note which said, "Smile. You do matter, and you are loved." She couldn't help but smile, and as she headed down the hall to class in the other direction, she lifted her head up and said "Hello" to two freshman girls.

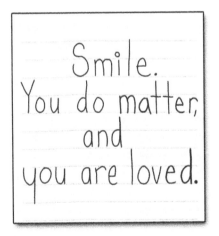

Chapter 8:
Jennifer and Mike Impact Others

As Mike filled his water bottle, he overheard two of the varsity basketball players talking. The first player said, "It doesn't look like I'm going to get any playing time this year."

The other player responded, "Me neither, I haven't even been getting much time in practice so far either."

The first player replied, "I just wish there was something I could do to help the team more."

Even though he knew he was eavesdropping, Mike felt this was an opportunity for him to help. "Hey guys. I don't know if it helps, but what about treating practice as if it were a game and bringing as much positive energy to help inspire the rest of your teammates?"

"What do you mean?" the second player asked.

"Obviously you have to continue to give your best effort whenever you get a chance to play in either practice or the game. But when you are on the sidelines, what about being more vocal, and positively encouraging the team?" Mike asked.

"Do you really think that would help?" the first player asked.

"I do." Mike responded. "Positive energy is contagious, and maybe if the team catches some of your positive energy and fire in practice the coach might take notice."

"POSITIVE ENERGY IS CONTAGIOUS"

"That could work," the second player replied. "It's worth a shot."

"My father always talks about working hard and bringing your best attitude and effort every day," the first player said.

"Thanks Mike! I appreciate you saying something," the first player said.

"Me too," the second player says, "we have to get to practice, see you later."

Although Mike was still disappointed he didn't make the varsity team, he was happy to try and help the team in any way he could. When the two varsity players were out of sight, he took two "Positivity Notes" from his pocket to leave for both players. His message was simple, but deep down inside he knew it could help. He wrote the same thing on each note "Spread Positive Energy, It Works!"

Spread Positive Energy, It Works!

After he placed one note in each player's locker, he turned around and noticed Jennifer standing about five feet away with a huge smile on her face.

"How long were you standing there?" Mike asked.

"Long enough to see you work your magic," Jennifer winked. "I am really proud of you Mike.

"I AM REALLY PROUD OF YOU"

I was actually looking for you when I saw you talking to those two players. Last night when we were looking up quotes and I found this one for you, and I think now is the perfect time to give it to you."

Jennifer handed Mike the "Positivity Note" that had a quote on it by Zig Ziglar. "Failure is an event, not a person."

> "Failure is an
> event, not a
> Person"
>   -Zig Ziglar-

Mike read the note twice before he turned to Jennifer, "Thanks, but I definitely feel like a failure for not making the varsity team. I really thought I had it."

"Mike, you know I am not really into sports, but remember how my grandfather used to always talk about boxing?" Jennifer asked.

Mike laughed, "He was always talking about the science of boxing and how it wasn't just the ultimate test of sport, but also the mind."

"He was such a great guy. He truly believed that boxing was extremely similar to life. He constantly stressed to my brother and I that 'you never lost a fight if you got knocked down – you only lost if you didn't get back up." Jennifer replied.

"I don't think I've ever thought about it like that," Mike said while nodding his head.

"Mike, I know you wanted to make Varsity this year. I am sorry you didn't. I know how hard you have worked. But not making the Varsity basketball team doesn't make you a failure, it only means that you failed to realize your goal this year," Jennifer responded.

"Thanks Jennifer, I really needed that," Mike said sincerely.

"You got it, Mike, I hope you know I'm always here for you,"

"I got to go" Mike abruptly shot back. "JV practice doesn't start for 25 minutes, but I want to get some extra work in. Thank you," Mike said over his shoulder and took off down the hallway heading toward the locker room to change.

Chapter 9:

Pete and His Father

While Pete was sitting alone outside his cell phone rang. It was his father. He didn't want to pick it up, but something inside him told him to answer.

"Hey dad," Pete said, answering the phone.

"Hey Pete, how are you doing buddy?" His father quietly asked.

His father only typically calls him buddy when something is wrong. "What's wrong?" Pete asked.

"I'm fine," his father says gently. "I just miss you, and I wanted to hear your voice. That's all. I wasn't sure if I was going to catch you, but I am glad I did. I know things between your mother and I are in a very difficult place right now, but I just wanted to tell you that I love you son, and I miss you."

A bit taken aback; Pete responds, "I love you too. I'll talk to you later."

"I LOVE YOU"

"Goodbye son," his father said softly as both of them hang up.

For the first time since his parents had begun the divorce process, Pete thought about his dad and what he must be feeling right now. His father moved out very abruptly and left the house for Pete and his mother, but he hadn't thought about how difficult that must have been for his father.

He heard his mother's side of things and heard her cry in her room at night. Pete decided to take a bold stance and he opened up his phone. He began writing a text message to both his mother and his father.

"Mom and Dad – I am writing to both of you because I want you to know that I love you both very much. I also know that everything is eventually going to be ok. I know you are both upset and hurt, but I am hoping you can try and figure out a way to get through this divorce in a more civil way. Love your son, Pete."

He was about to put his phone in his pocket when his mother responded and wrote: *"Thank you Pete."* Pete's father also responded with, *"I am proud of you, son."*

Pete smiled and let out his breath, he put his phone back in his pocket and headed towards the bus. In the back of his mind he had always hoped that his parents could eventually become friends again. Perhaps this could be the start.

Chapter 10:

The Spreading of Positivity Continues

For the next couple of weeks everywhere that Jennifer, Mike, and Pete went not only were they spreading their "Positivity Notes," but they were encouraging and lifting other people up whenever they could. It became a fun competitive game between the three of them, as they were continually recruiting more people into their Positivity Tribe each day.

Pete and Mike were walking down the hall one afternoon and were surprised to find "Positivity Notes" placed all throughout the hall, and they couldn't help but smile. There were notes posted on bulletin boards, inside as well as on the outside of lockers, in the classrooms, and they both noticed two freshman girls distributing their own positivity notes before class.

Mike looked to Pete as they were heading to their U.S. History class and said, "You know, I can feel a real sense of positive change here, and I am really proud of what Jennifer, you and I have been a part of."

"Me too, my man. At first, I wasn't sure where this was all going, but it's really taken off in a pretty cool way."

"In my free period yesterday, I was thinking about the impact we've had on other people. It's not just them. When I didn't make the Varsity Basketball team I was really depressed, but this whole positivity movement has been a very productive outlet." Mike said.

"I'm really proud of you Mike. You took something negative and you are now paying it forward to others in a very positive way." Pete said.

"Table that idea for a second, my man, because I am really proud of you too. Your parent's divorce I know has been very painful for both you and them, but amidst that challenge, you still found time to pay it forward in your own special way." Mike said proudly.

"Thanks, man, that means a lot," Pete said sincerely.

"Ya know Pete, we both mentioned 'paying it forward,' and it just hit me. Of course, it feels good to pay it forward to other people, and I love seeing their reaction… but it makes me feel even better in return." Mike said.

"PAYING IT FORWARD"

"I couldn't agree more man. The three of us have clearly had our challenges this year, but genuinely encouraging other people really feels good."

With that, Mike stopped in his tracks, and asked Pete, "How long until class?"

Looking down at his watch Pete said, "12 minutes, exactly."

"Perfect, let's grab a couple of 'Positivity Notes' and leave them in the kitchen for the morning staff tomorrow," Mike said.

"Dude, that's awesome! Let's go," Pete said. Mike and Pete took off down the hall to continue to pay it forward in their own special way. They knew the kitchen staff would arrive early before school, and they wanted them to feel appreciated and pleasantly surprised when they got to school tomorrow morning.

Chapter 11:
Mike Earns His Opportunity

Mike decided to stick around after JV practice finished to put in some extra work. The gym was completely empty. The conversation he had with Jennifer a few days earlier really had a positive impact on him and he was determined to continue to work hard. Even though he wasn't on varsity this year, he knew that he could still have a great JV season.

After running a couple extra sprints Mike decided to work on his foul shots. Out of the twenty he took, he made eighteen. After grabbing the last rebound he put the ball down next to him and he decided to run two more sprints. When he finished his last sprint, he hustled back to the foul-line. He heard footsteps behind him. Mike turned his head and saw the Varsity Head Coach, Mr. Meyers, approaching.

"Hey Mike, how was practice?" he asked.

"It was good, Coach," Mike answered.

"Mike, I am really proud of you... I know you were disappointed that you didn't make the varsity team this year, but I've been noticing your positive attitude as well as your work ethic." Coach said.

"Thanks Coach. That means a lot," Mike said proudly.

"Which brings me to my next point. Two of my players told me what you shared with them about positive energy. Since that day the two of them have not only lifted up their individual efforts, but their positive energy and attitude has been contagious with the entire team. This past week has been our best week of practice all season. I'd like you to join us and start practicing with our team tomorrow. How does that sound?" Coach asked.

"That sounds great Coach, but what about the JV team?" Mike asked.

"I would like you to play both. You are developing into a great leader and you have become such a positive mentor for the JV team. I think you will really add a lot to our varsity practices as well," Coach said.

"That works, Coach, thank you!" Mike replied, surprised and excited.

"The reason I wanted you to play on the JV team this year was to further develop you both as a player, as well as a leader. I believe in you Mike, and I know you are truly destined for greatness, not just on the basketball court but also in life."

"I BELIEVE IN YOU"

Mike was a bit taken aback by his coach's powerfully positive words, but he also felt extremely proud.

"You finish your JV season strong, and please continue to bring that positively contagious energy, spirit, and attitude to our varsity practices. Deal?" Coach asked.

"Deal!" Mike said enthusiastically. "You can count on me!"

"Great. And I'll see you tomorrow at practice." Coach replied.

"You got it Coach. Goodnight." Mike said with a smile.

Mike jogged back to the foul-line and made seven straight free-throws. He paused for a couple of moments to reflect. It was only two short months ago when he had pondered quitting basketball all together rather than playing another season on the JV team. Mike couldn't help but smile. Even though he hadn't made varsity this year, his positive attitude was making a difference in both his life and others. Tomorrow was going to be his first varsity practice, and he wanted to be ready. He immediately thought of a quote by Roger Staubach his father must have said a thousand times. "There are no traffic jams along the extra mile."

"There Are No Traffic Jams Along the Extra Mile" -Roger Staubach

Mike made four free-throws in a row. He ran over to his phone and opened up the notes section. He wanted to make sure that he used that quote for future "Positivity Notes."

Chapter 12:
Positivity in the Community

That Wednesday afternoon after lunch, Jennifer, Mike, and Pete were talking to nine other students in the hallway. They were laughing and having fun when Jennifer turned to everyone and said, "You know what today is right?"

"The day after yesterday," one student joked as he high-fived one of his friends.

"Nice try. It's actually Community Service Wednesday." Jennifer said. "We've had such an awesome and extremely Positive Impact throughout West Gordon High School, it would be fun if we decided to spread some Positivity throughout Bedford Hills."

"That sounds like a pretty cool idea, I'm in." one of the girls responded.

"What did you have in mind?" Mike asked.

"Well there's twelve of us in total so let's split up in three groups of four." Jennifer started.

"Let's spread positivity notes all over the Fire Station, the hospital, and why don't you and your group, Jennifer, head to the senior home." Pete suggested.

"That works," Jennifer said.

"We'll take the hospital, and we're going to put notes all over the staff, doctor and nurses parking lots." Mike said.

"That's awesome. We'll get the fire station, and we will try and get the fire trucks as well as the firemen's personal cars. Maybe we can add something personal like 'Thank you for your service' to those notes." Pete followed.

"That is a great idea. When we go to the nursing home, we'll see if we can get the staff to put positivity notes on each breakfast tray tomorrow, so they start their day off with some smiles." Jennifer said.

"Guys, this is really cool," one of the girls said. "I am really glad to be part of this."

"Let's get going," Mike said.

"But wait. Everyone's hand in, and 'Positivity' on three," Pete said.

With that, everyone put their hands in the center and shouted, "one, two, three…. POSITIVITY!"

"THE POWER OF POSITIVITY"

"Hey guys," Jennifer said to Pete and Mike. She held out her fists and gave them each a loving smile and a pound. The twelve students ran off to spread positivity throughout the community for the rest of that afternoon.

Chapter 13:

One Person at a Time

As Mike drove home that afternoon, he had a huge smile on his face. Mike couldn't wait to tell his parents about the positivity that he and his friends had spread that afternoon. As he was dancing to the latest Eminem song, he came to a pretty cool realization… he now understood that every single person has the potential to genuinely have a positive impact on other people. His mind wandered, and he kept on thinking out loud… eventually, he said to himself "Imagine if every person tried to positively impact just one person every single day. That positive impact would be incredible!" With a huge punch into his left palm, he turned the music up, rolled down both of his front windows and drove home with a huge smile on his face. As he parked, he took out his notebook and wrote down a couple of notes.

If every single person decided to spread positivity and inspire just one person every single day, the world would be a much better place.

Individually we can do a lot, but Together we ARE UNSTOPPABLE.

Together is a very Powerful word.

Chapter 14:
Jennifer Inspires Others

On Monday morning Jennifer happened to be walking down the freshman hall and she peered into Mr. Jackson's classroom. She remembers how difficult his English exams were as she saw him passing out the light blue notebooks for one of his famous and almost impossible exams. She walked into the classroom with a bunch of "Positivity Notes" in her hand and greeted Mr. Jackson.

"Hi Jennifer, what brings you here?" He asked.

"Well, I saw you handing out your test notebooks, and well—I was wondering if I could leave a "Positivity Note" on everyone's desk before the students arrive?"

"I don't see why not. Maybe it will help inspire their creativity," he said with a wink.

Jennifer proceeded to place one "Positivity Note" on top of each of the light blue exam books. She couldn't help but smile, as she hoped it would have a positive impact on the students before the exam. As she was placing the last note and walking out, the freshman students began arriving. In her head she couldn't help but think "I hope these notes make a difference for just one person."

Chapter 15:
Muting Negativity

Pete was sitting on his bed scrolling through his Instagram account.

He couldn't help but notice that so many of his friends easily spread negativity on social media. One friend would comment by leaving either a teasing or negative comment and so many others would immediately like it and share it. He continued to scroll for a couple more minutes until he paused for a moment and quietly placed his cell phone down on his bed. Pete sat there in silence just thinking for a couple of moments. He decided he was going to figure out a way to mute negativity by spreading positivity.

"MUTE NEGATIVITY BY SPREADING POSITIVITY"

Without hesitating he opened his personal Instagram page and scrolled down to the settings. He clicked the delete button. A warning notice popped up - "Are you sure you want to delete this account? It is permanent, and you will lose all data." Again, without hesitation he clicked "accept," and his Instagram account was gone. He wanted a fresh start. Pete smiled and clicked on the "add new account" button. Within two minutes he had created the account for "The Positivity Tribe" (The.Positivity.Tribe). He knew exactly what he wanted to share for his first post and story. He leaned over and grabbed his notebook. He was going to use one of his all-time favorite quotes by Mahatma Gandhi, "Be the change you want to see in the world."

Chapter 16:
7-Point Creed

Jennifer was sitting at her desk in front of her computer.

She was supposed to be typing up a paper for English class, but she just wasn't into it. Her mind was somewhere else. She couldn't help thinking back to this same time last year when she was being bullied pretty badly. She couldn't understand it at the time, but now she truly realized that when people are hurt or hurting, they often lash out at others. Frequently that pain is misdirected toward innocent people that have not caused any of their pain or suffering. Although she wasn't able or willing to understand it at the time, she now grasped both the value and truth in it today. One thing she was always proud of, is how she didn't fight back. At times she wanted to, but she knew that her parents had taught her strong values. As she was sitting at her desk, still unable to get into her English assignment, she had an idea and opened up a brand-new blank document. She titled it "The 7-Point Creed."

She grabbed her notebook to look at her notes over the last few weeks and she opened it up to a page from last week and began typing...

BE KIND, BE POSITIVE, BE GRATEFUL, BE ENCOURAGING, BE HUMBLE, BE GENEROUS AND BE FORGIVING.

BE KIND
BE POSITIVE
BE GRATEFUL
BE ENCOURAGING
BE HUMBLE
BE GENEROUS
BE FORGIVING

She sat back in her chair and looked at that list for a couple of minutes. She loved it! There wasn't anything she wanted to change. She hit print three times and walked over to her printer. She was going to keep one sheet for herself, and she was super excited to give one to both Pete and Mike tomorrow on the bus. She glanced at her cell phone and the time read 9:46 PM. She had dillydallied enough. Now it was time for her to finish her English assignment. To echo one of the 7-Point Creeds, she said out loud and confidently "BE POSITIVE," and sat down to finally start her English assignment.

Chapter 17:
Parents Jump on Board

On Friday Jennifer's parents were over having dinner with Mike's parents at their house. The evening was going well, and both couples were having a really nice time. After dinner was finished Mike's mother suggested they take the evening into the living room. Mike's father followed carrying a large box. He quietly picked up his glass, "I would like to make a toast." Both his wife and Jennifer's parents picked up their glasses.

"Over these past three to four months, I have witnessed the incredible positive change that Jennifer, Mike, and Pete have all had. I am so proud of how the three of them have had such a positive impact on both their school as well as our community. Well," he brushed a tear from the corner of his eye, "Mike has been such a positive force within our family, helping us to always look at the bright side."

Mike's mother put her hand on her husband's shoulder and stood up to take over. "What I think my husband is trying to say is that we would like to raise our glasses to three incredible teenagers."

With that, all four parents clinked their glasses, "Cheers!"

Michael's father walked over to the box and pointed to it,

"I have one more little surprise also. As you guys know I run a marketing and advertising agency here in Bedford Hills, and, well I would like to give these to Jennifer, Mike, and Pete." With that, he reached into the box and pulled out small white pads.

The Positivity Tribe

Join Our
"Pay it Forward with
   Positivity Mission"

Post your note on Instagram
and tag The.Positivity.Tribe to
help spread the positivity!
TO YOUR GREATNESS!

Mike's father continued, "I know it's not much, but it's our way as parents to help our kids follow their passion in spreading positivity." With that, all four parents stood and exchanged hugs.

Jennifer's mother added, "You know, this is not only incredibly generous, but the kids are going to love them. Thank you very much."

Jennifer's father continued, "I think it would be really special if we each wrote some "Positivity Notes" of our own."

"That's a great idea," Mike's mom said with a huge smile

on her face. Mike's father handed out a pad as well as a Sharpie to each of the parents.

Chapter 18:
The Importance of Gratitude

Jennifer, Mike, and Pete sat at the kitchen table in Jennifer's house. Jennifer jumps up from the table and says, "I have something for the three of us," and quickly runs into the next room. "Close your eyes." As both Mike and Pete closed their eyes Jennifer came back into the room holding something in each of her hands. She said, "Open up" and handed Mike and Pete their own Positivity Tribe bracelets complete with the #werisebyliftingothersup inscribed on them.

"These are awesome, thank you," Mike said, slipping his on.

While putting his on, Pete said, "I'm never taking mine off."

Before he was about to ask if she had one, Pete looked at Jennifer's right wrist and saw that she had her own bracelet on also.

Mike quickly stood up from the kitchen table and reached into his backpack. "You are not the only one with a surprise," he handed both Jennifer and Pete one of the "Positivity Notepads" his father had shown Jennifer's parents the night before.

"These are so awesome!" Jennifer exclaimed.

"Dude – these rock!" Pete shouted.

The three of them passed the notes around for a couple of minutes and just enjoyed each other's company as they began filling out the notes with more quotes together.

Pete decided it was his turn, so he turned around to grab something out of his book bag. When he turned around, he had two things for both Jennifer and Mike in his hands. What Jennifer didn't know was that a few weeks ago when she handed both Mike and Pete the 7-Point Creed it really had a profound impact on Pete. Pete not only looked at the list each day, but he made it part of his daily affirmations. Pete handed both Mike and Jennifer each a laminated 7-Point Creed, as well as a sticker of the 7-Point Creed in cool, red black and white colors.

"Jennifer, I don't think you understand the impact your 7-Point Creed had on me but thank you" Pete said sincerely.

"Well, first off, thank you Pete but it's not MY 7-Point Creed, it's OUR 7-Point Creed," she said with both a smile and a wink.

"Well I have to say thank you so much for sharing that with Mike and I, and I am really glad you said it was our creed." Pete responded.

"I am stunned," Jennifer said, "thank you."

"Ya, this is really cool Pete; I am going to put the sticker on the cover of my journal so I can see it every single day." Mike responded.

"Guys, I would like to say a very sincere thank you to both of you. My junior year was becoming painful, but together we were able to really turn it around. You two are my best friends, and I love you both," she said as she leaned in and gave both of them a group hug.

"No way! It's Mike and I that owe you our sincere gratitude," Pete responded.

"Ya, he's right. Thank you so much for everything you did." Mike said.

"Now you are really going to make me cry," Jennifer said. "But you guys helped me too, in more ways than you know."

With a sincere look on his face, Mike asked something that really shocked both Jennifer and Pete. "Have you two ever really thought about all that happened this year?"

"Probably more than you know," Pete said.

"Definitely. This was both the best and the worst year," Jennifer quietly commented.

"What do you mean?" Pete shot back.

"The constant bullying was really beginning to take its toll on me. There were times I felt alone, but you both were really there for me, and we became even closer."

"My parents' divorce has been extremely painful this past year. I clearly love them both very much, but at times I honestly felt like running away." Pete said with a tear in his eye.

"Guys, I don't know if this makes sense, but I don't think any of this actually happened TO us." Mike responded.

"Huh?" Jennifer asked a she tilted her head with a very confused look on her face.

"I think all of this actually happened FOR us," Mike said, almost not believing himself. "If I didn't get cut from the team, if your parents weren't going through their divorce, and if you hadn't been bullied – I don't think the three of us would be having this conversation right now. I also don't think we would have created this positive movement or The Positivity Tribe."

"Wait a second. I think I get what you are saying. Don't get me wrong, some of what we went through was both incredibly painful and difficult, but I think you are right." Pete said, almost convinced.

"And as we were going through it, we went through it together, and we did it as positively as we could," Jennifer said confidently.

"Exactly! It didn't take away the pain, but it led us to where we are today." Mike said.

"And I wouldn't trade that for anything," Pete said, smiling.

"These things didn't happen to us, they actually happened for us." Jennifer repeated.

"THINGS DON'T HAPPEN TO US, THEY HAPPEN FOR US"

"I am so grateful that the two of you were there for me, and I am so glad we went through this together." Mike said.

"Me too," Pete said. "Me too."

"The power of gratitude," Jennifer said.

"And the power of positivity," Mike followed.

"And the power of love," Pete added.

Jennifer leaned over and gave Mike a huge hug. She whispered in his ear "I love you." She then walked over to Pete and also gave him a giant hug as she whispered, "I love you, Pete."

Chapter 19:

One Year Later – High School Graduation

Principal Jefferson stood at the podium and addressed the murmuring crowd. "We have one final award of recognition that I would like to present. This award goes to three individuals that have single-handedly had a profound impact on the culture of West Gordon High School. From the faculty to the students and parents, in the classroom and on the sports field—there is not a single person that these three individuals have not positively impacted in some way. When it comes to their motto, 'We rise by lifting others up,' their reach will continue to expand way beyond our school and our community, and I can't thank them enough. With that said, it gives me the absolute honor to present the first-ever Positivity Tribe Award to Jennifer Jordan, Mike Pollard, and Pete Wooden."

The crowd rose to their feet in a very loud and raucous cheer as they applauded for Jennifer, Mike, and Pete. The three of them looked at each other and smiled as they stood. Mike turned to Jennifer and Pete and said, "This is just the beginning."

As the three of them walked to the stage they noticed the janitor, Mr. Williams, to their immediate right. He was clapping for them with a giant smile on his face. Jennifer, Mike, and Pete smiled back. While they were still looking directly at him, Mr. Williams reached into his front shirt pocket and pulled a couple of the original "Positivity Notes" the three of them found in their locker one year ago. Mr. Williams winked at the three of them and mouthed the words "I'm proud of you."

With a surprised look on their faces Jennifer, Mike, and Pete smiled, nodded, and mouthed back "Thank you," as they continued walking. The three of them accepted their awards together.

Jennifer, Mike, and Pete headed back to their seats with their awards in hand. Mike looked at Jennifer and Pete with a proud smile on his face. He paused for a couple of seconds to reflect and take the moment in. He turned toward Jennifer and Pete and gave each of them a fist bump and said, "The power of positivity…one person at a time."

THE END

Acknowledgements

We would like to recognize and acknowledge some very influential people that helped make this book a reality. First off, we need to say a very special thank you to Dominick Domasky and Motivation Champs. You have been extremely influential and supportive throughout this entire process and we truly appreciate both your guidance as well as your friendship.

We would also like to thank Laura Edgerly, Cody Sims, Bethany Votaw and Lynn Wagner. The four of you have been fantastic to work with, and we truly appreciate all of your work and effort behind the scenes.

About the Author:
Christopher J. Wirth

Christopher J. Wirth is the founder and president of No Quit Living. As a professional speaker, coach and trainer, Christopher works with individuals, sports teams and corporations to help improve accountability, effectiveness, and efficiency through his process – "The Positive Mental Advantage."

Christopher is the host of the No Quit Living Podcast, which has been rated as a top 50 Podcast on iTunes in three different categories; Business, Health, and Self-Help.

Christopher is also the founder of The Positivity Tribe, a coaching, speaking and training company that focuses on working with schools, sports teams and organizations looking to adopt both a Positive Mindset and Positive Advantage.

Christopher has coached Basketball at the High School and Collegiate Levels. In addition he coached an AAU Team that succeeded at the National Level.

Christopher graduated from Washington College with a BA in both Business Management and Drama. Christopher was a member of both the Men's Basketball and Tennis teams.

Christopher has three children, Zachary, Emily and Mason.

About the Author:

Chris Wilberding

Chris's passion for helping individuals achieve their personal and professional goals started as a social studies teacher and men's college basketball coach. This passion carried over to an extremely successful 25+ year career in the field of proprietary education focused primarily on start-up and turnaround opportunities. Throughout his professional career, Chris has had some level of positive impact on the lives of well over 100,000 students.

Throughout his career, he has excelled in establishing positive and engaging environments for people to become the best versions of themselves. As part of this, he has developed on-going accountability models for academic, athletic, and corporate teams focused on driving individual and ultimately team success. These experiences have resulted in Chris bringing his passion project to life as the Founder of The 419 Project.

As the co-author of The Positivity Tribe, Chris looks forward to positively impacting others—one person at a time.

Fundamentally, Chris believes that **PEOPLE** are put on this earth with one sole **PURPOSE** and gain their greatest happiness when their **PASSION** impacts others in a **POSITIVE** way.

Connect With the Positivity Tribe

To hire The Positivity Tribe to Speak or work with you, your team, company or school visit:
www.thepositivitytribe.com

Themes from The Positivity Tribe:

The Power of Positivity

WE Rise By Lifting Others Up

Positive Energy is Contagious

Pay IT Forward

Things Don't Happen To Us, They Happen FOR Us

Gratitude

I am Proud of You

I Love You

The Positivity Tribes 7-Point Creed:

BE Kind

BE Positive

BE Grateful

BE Encouraging

BE Humble

BE Generous

BE Forgiving

CPSIA information can be obtained
at www.ICGtesting.com
Printed in the USA
FSHW010246050221
78235FS